No Longer Bound

ADREAN MASON

Copyright © 2020 Adrean Mason

All rights reserved.

ISBN: 9798665545714

Table of Contents

LETTER FROM THE AUTHOR

1	Chapter 1 — DECIDE TO WIN ANYWAY	1
2	Chapter 2 — SHAKE YOURSELF LOOSE	11
3	Chapter 3 — DISEASE TO DESIGN	17
4	Chapter 4 — ENCOUNTER AND EXPERIENCE	21
5	Chapter 5 — PRISON TO PASSION	27
6	Chapter 6 — THE MOVIE THAT LASTS A LIFETIME	33
7	Chapter 7 — FROM SOMEONE THAT KNOWS	39
8	Chapter 8 — IT HAPPENS OVER TIME	43
9	Chapter 9 — V: VIOLATION	47
10	Chapter 10— I: ISOLATION	53
11	Chapter 11— C: COMFORTLESS	59
12	Chapter 12— T: TOILING	63
13	Chapter 13— I: INSANITY	67
14	Chapter 14— M: MOUNTAINS	71
15	Chapter 15— FORCE IN ACTION	75

ABOUT THE AUTHOR   77

LETTER FROM THE AUTHOR

Secret Sin

Sexual Abuse
Abuse occurs between ages 4 -18
(Molestation / Attempted Rape / Rape)
1 out of every 9 girls
1 out of every 53 boys

The effects of child sexual abuse can be long lasting and affect the victim's mental health.

Victims are more likely than non-victims to experience mental health challenges:

- 4 times more likely to develop symptoms of Drug Abuse
- 4 times more likely to experience PTSD as an adult
- 3 times more likely to experience major Depressive Episode as an adult

Secret Sin

Why are we not talking about this aloud!
I'm a witness, and the statistics support, that you or someone you know in your close-knit circle, including your family, is a victim.

"No Longer Bound" is a true account and testimony of the internal battles that, if unchallenged, can hold you captive and bind you from success and true happiness.

Don't delay, order your copies today! Send them out as gifts and as keys that unlock wisdom and revelation waiting to be unleashed.

Those you work with, dine with, even go to church with, need you to order today! Many lives, your friends, and quite a strong possibility, your family member, are all waiting on you! If only we would be bold and courageous, stand up to reveal and confront the secret sin!

You Help me reveal it each time you share this book, "No Longer Bound" is the one simple gesture that will pierce massive holes in darkness. Each time the book is read and shared, the adversary loses his grip, and ropes of bondage are broken and falls off the victim.

My prayer is for all those who suffered from the hand of this secret sin is to be set free and live life unhindered! They will join the fight and help set others free!

This book is intended for all victims: male and female. It is recommended for all audiences of any size: an individual, a group, you may be related to the victim, family member, or friend. It is inspirational for any book club, counseling session, group therapy, church study session, and support groups.

Order several copies today, one for yourself, and each of your friends. Read it together, it's a great read for all ages from young teens to any age adult. Counselors would agree, "No Longer Bound" is relatable to all ages and relevant for the untold stories of today.

This world is filled with so much darkness. Help expose this secret sin and dispel the darkness!

Each of us have been called to fight for others. You are strong and have been equipped to help those that have been wounded, bruised, and bound.

Always remember, the more we spread the Word and share our testimonies, we expose darkness and decay, close the gap between the have and have nots and begin to live victoriously!

Help the lives of others live "No Longer Bound"!

Signed Adrean Mason

ADREAN MASON

CHAPTER 1
DECIDE TO WIN ANYWAY

My first memory of being alive is dark, demented, and twisted; a haunting memory that would never leave the corridors of my heart, nor the windows of my mind. This world, and my life in it, have taught me; these memories would painstakingly grow with me and try its best efforts to cast its dark shadow over my every individual step of every waking moment, and even un-waking (yes, I just made up a new word that means when I am asleep in my dreams). What it did not want me to know is that it could only haunt me and overshadow me as I allow it. Basically, we all have a say in the matter. What we say about it will cast the shadow. What we do about it, will determine how long we live in the shadows.

Some scholars refer to "life" as a race to be run with all diligence and hope, a race that one would have hope of winning. Really!? How can I win a race that even before I was shown "On the Mark", even before I could and would "Get Set", and listen out to hear the shout of "The Go", I was beaten breathless, wounded and crippled lame? I was left near dead, dead to the idea that winning may be for some, but surely it was not for me.

Kill a man, you only stop the one man from thriving, but he lives on through the lives of others. Kill the man's idea, you stop the masses from existing and thriving! I am not dead; I am alive, and I have embraced the idea that I do win! Not only do I win, I will help the masses learn how they are designed to win as well. It is my belief, contrary as it may be to the world, that the world has opposing forces and these forces can be traced back to the ruler of darkness, dark powers, principalities, spiritual wickedness in low and high places.

I believe in good versus evil, protagonists always fought the antagonist. I believe in heaven and hell; I believe there are little "g" gods, witches and warlocks, I also believe there is The Most High GOD, His name is YHWH, who art in heaven, hallowed be His Name! And there is also a devil who thinks of himself as a god. His name is Satan, and he holds no real power compared to GOD. In fact, Satan was kicked out of heaven for being jealous and trying to override and gain the Sovereignty of YHWH.

When he was kicked out, only a third of the angels went with him. It is my belief that no matter what he conjures up and makes his best effort to control and manipulate, he is no match for YHWH! It is my clear understanding, Satan and his kingdom set up shop on this earth, and history proves him, with all of his deception, tricks, vices, and lies, actually effective. It has proven to be highly effective in what he does to lure people away from the truth and love of YHWH that causes them to give up on the idea of winning and forfeit the race. I know this by personal experience. I almost gave up.

If you knew the story, some would even say, "Satan sure enough had her out for the count," and he left me for blind to hope, bankrupt in my soul, weighted down with a feeling of unquenchable drought to the idea that I could actually win. Boyyyy was he wrong. Satan underestimated the value of restored and renewed purpose, my God-given purpose.

Satan's twisted plot to get me to do as he did, ditch reverence for GOD ALMIGHTY and trade it for "g" god status, did not work! His plot to kill, steal, and destroy has only given me fortitude in my purpose and plan to exist and thrive! He may have invaded my world, my life as a 4 year-old, but now, I am nearly fifty, and the time that has transpired has been a blessing and not his intended curse.

My life and my living it will not be in vain! I have found favor in the time. Time has been on my side. I have learned over the span of time that time is a gift from YHWH. This gift has supernatural elements that would come to reveal an irrevocable power that leads to the real truth. The truth that perpetuates an uncompromised synergy that leads to a wholeness that includes, but not limited to, forgiveness that creates healing from the knowledge gleaned and gained from the infallible Word and Presence of YHWH, and wisdom that brings about an understanding and transformational revelation that ultimately grafts you into a woven love relationship with YHWH. It, most importantly, induces a reverence for the Creator of time Himself, YHWH.

YHWH, The Great I Am, Creator of the universe, heaven, and earth, the seen and the unseen. YHWH is ELOHIM, The Holy Trinity in His fullness, GOD THE FATHER (YHWH), GOD THE SON (YAHUSHUA HAMASHIACH), GOD THE HOLY SPIRIT (RUACH). I am convinced and experienced enough to know a few things about this life in this so-called world. Here on earth, YHWH created with an original plan in mind, and since the beginning of creation, the instruction has not changed.

Mankind (man and woman) have their place in

the plan. We (man and woman) are responsible for certain things such as: subdue, have dominion, be fruitful and multiply. Frankly, I need you to accept that there are opposing forces and opposers, whose that mere existence is to stop you from becoming and completing your assignment of subduing, having dominion, being fruitful and multiplying. So, the opposition is often times a stealth operation to kill, steal, and destroy the idea and hope that you can and will win. Please read that again if necessary.

I need you to get the fact that, most often, the stealth operation was designed to get you distracted or stretched thin and thinking that the opposition is your very own, personal, shortcoming, and there is nothing you can do to overcome and just to accept them. STOP! Do not believe the lies! Knock off the weight of the lies, set yourself free. Face the lies. Stand up to them and knock them off of you!

We will never really know the countless numbers of lives that prematurely expire without realizing their full potential. Some expire in old age and untapped potential. Some left this world in youthful years and untapped potential. The common thread is that they lived and died underneath and short of their intended potential. Underdeveloped talents and gifts that stayed hidden went back to the dust of the graves with them. The world was supposed to be enhanced and enriched because of them. Many would say that they died before it was their time.

I get it, I fully understand how exhausting this type of life would be. I can relate to the disastrous, dramatic ending of many of the lives that unfortunately ended prematurely. Today, we have witnessed so many succumb to the exhaustion. This exhaustion has no picks nor favorites, or certain status, socioeconomic influence. Every created being is on its radar.

We've seen the news reports, a hanging by one's own hand, a drug overdose in a hotel room, a drowning, a drunkard car collision, all lives evaporated and reduced to pain that drove the owner of the life to seek refuge in death. The death certificates should all read, "death by deception". I am angered by such loss. How is that an answer? I do not speak from a place of judgment, but from a place of familiarity. How is it that the horror of taking your own life is more seductive than living through the pain? Emphasis on "living through".

I remember the pain and feeling like I could not escape it, so I understand why people choose ways of escaping that turn out to be traps to self-destruction, an early grave filled with untapped potential. I made it out of the traps. I am so grateful that I made it free of the traps, but my heart hurts for the masses that do not know how to break free of the traps of destruction. I now know the power in telling my story. I have broken my silence, and I am now set free and share with others how to win big anyway!

CHAPTER 2
SHAKE LOOSE

For many years, and even sometimes now, I would catch myself shaking my head trying to shake loose the daunting memories. I ponder all in the same breath, why am I shaking my head as though, if I actually shake my head hard enough, my brain would somehow shift the memories out of my head, out of my thoughts, and even out of my life. News flash: Not a chance! The memories are there and there to stay no doubt!

Will I, can I, ever wash away the residue of this pain, hurt, horror, and haunting memory that, I honestly confess, seem like it has hunted me like a bounty hunter hunts his greatest reward? This is the Million-dollar question that you ask yourself over and over until it becomes a broken record that will not stop! It is stuck on replay. Someone, anyone, please stop the replay!

Seriously …. think about it for a moment. Some of you will know exactly what I am explaining in this instance, the rest of you, I want you to imagine your worst sound. You know the nails on the chalk board type sound. The sound that invades your very core and drives you to the edge. Your personal cliff, that all it takes is for just one more defeat and, yep, you willingly plunge yourself off the cliff! Yeah, that sound! Well, I was introduced to my sound as a child, defenseless and innocent child. Now, as I approach fifty years old. I lived to tell the story, a story like so many had the potential of becoming a high-resolution pixel on the poster of victim.

Other than the fact that we live in a world filled with opposing forces designed to kill, steal, and destroy, I do not know why it happened to me. This is void of the fact that I am a created being created with a purpose that is connected to the lives of other created beings that the connection alone would create a synergetic force that cannot be reckoned with that defeats the opposer's plan.

It is important to know, before I reached that revelation, I was plagued by the "why me" question. The revelation led to a freedom, but believe you me, there was no freedom in my life prior to this revelation.

That was my premise of every failure, every defeat, every disconnect, heartbreak, argument, disagreement, abandonment, and rejection. Oh, my stars, just writing about the trappings of the that question is the very exhaustion that leads to self-destruction and to the destruction of others.

This thing has two avenues, it turns inward to you, for you to destroy yourself, or it turns outward, for you to destroy others. If it has complete, desired control, it does both! Ooooooo, you know exactly what I am talking about and, in this instant, as you are reading and will continue to read, your brain's library and extensive media records, of your life, is showing flash cards of the toxic relationships and incidents that you witnessed from afar. These took place at your home, in your school, at your workplace, at the bank, at the grocery store, in traffic, at the subway, on the bus, on the train, and on the plane.

You get me? You understand that the opposer is after ALL created human beings and wants to destroy our relationship of love, honor, and respect towards one another. He seeks to sever our connection to our loving Heavenly Father, ABBA Father! He has chosen to use his time to settle the score with all created beings because we, mankind, the created beings, were created as his replacement to commune and worship the LORD, thy YHWH. Created beings took his place to have a love and reverent relationship.

As I came to this understanding, its revelation opened the door for me. It explained and granted me forgiveness towards myself and others for all of the poor decisions that led to bad actions, the pretend life, make-believe happiness, dressed up wounds, drowning sorrows in fornication, alcohol, drugs, sex, lies, manipulation, pride, selfishness, self-righteousness, and the list goes on. I was able to embrace the liberty of forgiveness, and I forgave the abuse, neglect, abandonment, rejection, anxiety depression, and the ignorance of just not knowing any better.

I am free! I have been set free! I am certain that you have identified with me, and that your heart has even begun to access memories in hidden access files of your mind and heart. I encourage you today to be set free. Let RUACH, The Holy Spirit of our Living God, loose in the dark-filled corridors leading to your moment of attack and violation.

Do not stay in that hurt place alone, He will come and get you. Trust Him! Let His presence flush you out of that darkness. With the gentleness of His voice through the Holy Word, come to the light where there is healing and forgiveness that will culture your growth and restoration. It is time for your renewal and to be fully restored by the hand and might of ELOHIM. If you choose to stay in the dark, where unforgiveness and hate breeds, you could possibly get stuck in there and even die in there.

I understand, I was there not too long ago I, like you, sat guarding my gifts and talents, because I made a vow never to be hurt again and to protect myself. Do not let this fear control you, please. I understand your feeling of safety, that you have to stay inside in the dark behind the armored door with all of your gifts, and talents, inventions, and ideas scattered around you, dancing and never leaving your thoughts and dreams.

Come out from the shadows. Do not let it destroy you and what you are to become. I speak as a representative of created beings. We want and need you; your gifts, talents, and love, and connection are what only you can bring to this place we call world. Your presence is to help prepare this world for the heavenly Kingdom. You are part of the dress rehearsal… "on earth as it is in heaven"!

Like you, I had, had convinced myself to keep the real me hidden behind the shadows, and the one that will be visible to the world is a dressed up, pretend version. I will be completely honest and transparent with you when I say, it almost drove me over the edge. I had ten different nervous break downs, each one graduating in levels of intensity. Some involving armed policemen, sheriff escorts, and guarded rooms.

And, along the way in my race to plunge off a steep cliff, I picked up some unsightly hitchhikers (lol). I laugh, now, because I can, and this story is a story in retrospect, hindsight even, but along the way, it was no laughing matter. I considered myself an infectious disease, and with dark memories on replay, I was comfortable with dark and gloom and attracted those things that thrive in darkness, disease.

ADREAN MASON

CHAPTER 3
DISEASE TO DESIGN

I had been infected and had become a disease, spreading and infecting others until it was my turn to die. And I was okay with knowing that, but what I came to find out that some disease can mutate itself and build resistances that keeps it alive and spreading. I began to ask myself, *when will this end*, and when you do not get an answer, you begin to hypothesize and formulate your own answers. Hence, the destructive behaviors are born and extends into various shapes and sizes that it can manifest.

This was my metaphorical state of mind as a child, adolescent, teenager, young adult, single woman, unwed mother, unhappy married woman, and then middle-aged, divorced woman. The disease mutated, and its stench would spread throughout life's different stages of development, or the lack there of. That was my viewpoint until I encountered YAHUSHUA HAMASHIACH as my Redeemer! The only one that could love me beyond the stench of my grave and beyond the bondage of my faults.

My friend, you are my family because of HIM. I want to see you set free as I currently live. If you have not encountered HIM yet, I understand your hesitation and can tell you that it is caused by disbelief that was created from abuse, mistrust, hurt, pain, and unanswered questions. I record my story so that you know and feel you are not alone. I am right here with you, presently, and can take the journey with you back to the place of devastation. Let us walk out of there together!

It is important that you know that this freedom is for everyone who wants it and wants to learn how to be and live free. It sounds easy, but you know that it is not as easy as it sounds. No one wakes up or walks through life and says that they are going to be bound with the plan of destruction, corruption, and only the Lord knows what else.

My point is, you do not ask for it, but somehow, it finds you and wears you like a cheap suit.

I am certain that you agree with me that it is time to trade in this cheap suit for a tailored design!

ADREAN MASON

CHAPTER 4
ENCOUNTER AND EXPERIENCE

As old as I am, it was just recently that I had a real encounter with YHWH as my loving Father, ABBA. The lesson in this, it is never too late! HE has not forgotten you, despite your age or degree of circumstance. Even after the countless cries of desperations, I had no encounter. I can confidently say, from my experience and several women recorded in the bible, GOD is not moved by tears, rather, is moved by faith and commitment.

Despite the blessed reassurances in the songs, psalms, prayers, and chants of victory, I, along with my five senses, felt like a disease. Hear me when I say this, just tuck away these words into your heart, they will not come back void. It may not be of much use today, tomorrow next week, or next year, but rest assured, I testify that YAHUSHUA HAMASHIACH died on a cross and every word of my testimony and millions like me are the reason you will overcome.

YHWH is no respecter person, HE did it for me and has done it for you too. I share a confession to echo into the four winds surrounding you, audibly confess these words aloud into your atmosphere. "I truly belong to YHWH. HIS fullness as ELOHIM works on my behalf. HE has already made provision that will guide me through and walk me out of my grave, out of this darkness, through the valley, and shadows of death by doubt into HIS glorious light.

I will encounter HIM and HIS Presence. In an instant, I will know HE is loving, not judgmental. HE is patient and does not rush me. HE is not vindictive; HE is kind and has only the best for me in all areas of my life, now and to come. HE wants me to have an encounter with HIM!

HE wants to fill me with HIS love and liberty. HE trusts me to share my life of freedom, honor, blessings, and abundance. HE loves me without conditions, and HIS love is everlasting. HE saved me, saved me from a life of corruption and destruction. I once lived as a victim, and its introduction of pain and hurt became my induction to live as a victim. But now,

I am free, and free indeed. I am more than a conqueror! I am who I am because HE loves me! I am finally free to be!"

My eternal life has begun in my lifetime now! HalleluYAH! I know and feel the Father's Love for me as his daughter, precious to HIM, HIS beautiful, baby girl all grown up. HE is my Protector and wants and has the absolute best for me. HE looks at me and can see my future, and He knows what I am great in and what I will need lots of help in. HE has made big plans for me, great plans even. I am loving every day and what is unfolding and building for me!

HE knows my heart and sensitivities, my strengths, and opportunities. HE also knows my desires, the greatest to the least of them. HE has blessed and prepared my heart to live holy, satisfied, and whole in my devoted singleness, as well as a nurturing, devout wife. As either, I am the apple of HIS eye. (Praise Break!)

YHWH knows just how to get and to keep my attention. Some distractions are not always censored and flagged down like a computer malware program. Sometimes I benefit from the loudest bells and whistles, the brightest colors, melodies, songs, pictures, poems, HIS WORD and, even silence. HE knows how to redirect me back when I am lured off track, and I do get lured off.

I experience HIM daily and know that HIS Presence is alongside me, always, as is HIS Holy Spirit. RUACH is the Teacher and Principal in my life. YAHUSHUA is the Redeemer that made our road to redemption even possible. HE is mankind's ultimate sacrifice. HIS life, without sin, took on all mankind's sin, past, present, and future, to suffer the painful and gruesome death.

Nailed to the cross, He became sin and was separated from The Father to work out salvation for all that would accept him as personal savior. HE was the one punished, beat unrecognizably, and nailed to The Cross, so that mankind could, once again, fellowship with the Father and experience an intimacy like no other.

Folks, I give it to you this way, YAHUSHUA HAMASHIACH was not the first to be nailed to a cross, nor was HE the last, but HE, and HE alone, was THE ONLY ONE who could bridge the gap and reconnect man back to the Father. For He, alone, knew no sin, whose blood would be accepted before the Father on the Mercy Seat of the Holy of Holies. Amen! HE loves you; feel HIS love inside of a protected, personal, and very real relationship.

This personal, intimate relationship, I speak of, is not new to man. I repeat, it is not new to man, in fact, it was the first relationship ever experienced by the created human beings.

As an introduction to some, and a reminder to others, it's still the same account: Adam, is recorded in the book of Genesis as the first man created by YHWH, in HIS Fullness as ELOHIM. Adam experienced this beautiful, almost indescribable, fellowship and relationship with The Father, GOD Almighty HIMSELF! WOW! Until…dunt dunt duntttt, he disobeyed YHWH and followed the misguidance of his wife, Eve, who had been beguiled by the subtlety of the serpent.

Adam, through his own disobedience, ate of the forbidden fruit, severing his reverent relationship and communion with our Heavenly Father. This, as we know it, could only be restored through the one, acceptable sacrifice of YAHUSHUA HAMASHIACH. Good News everyone, YAHUSHUA HAMASHIACH did! (Praise Break!)

I am so grateful; no amount of words could add up to be sufficient to express proper gratitude of not being left disconnected.

ADREAN MASON

CHAPTER 5
FROM PRISON TO PASSION

Ladies and gentlemen, I was a goner; depressed, dark, twisted, confused, angry, bitter, resentful, jealous, and hopeless in the volume of my own strength. I was doing what I was bad enough to do. BUT YHWH pulled me up out of the quicksand of deception! HE rescued me countless times, when I began to drown in the sewage of my woes. Woes that may have started when I was a child, but I made certain that there were dozens more added and self-induced.

I had built my very own personal San Quintin. An island of isolation, imprisoned with the most dangerous, sentenced criminals of my past. YHWH came to my island and would not leave me, HE stayed right there with me, convincing me to just try HIM. HE would love me better than my momma. HE would love me better than any spouse. HE would never abandon me.

I was exhausted and had settled in on my island. I was so tired of pretending, dressing up my pain, my shame, and putting on a show, fooling everyone around me. Here is a neon, flashing light reminder, I could not fool and get away from myself. Eventually, it must come to an end.

After a while, you do not know who you are because you changed so regularly, depending upon your audience. I was becoming that thing in which I hated. Enough was enough! JESUSSSS are you real? I was finally ready to commit to a change.

My tears did not move Him, my commitment did. My commitment expressed that I am seeking HIM and that I need HIM to be real for me! No more forms of godliness, I was looking for a relationship that no man could give me. I was desperate for a real, core change, sending out S.O.S. signals for a search and rescue mission that only HE could answer.

Thank you to JESUS, my MESSIAH! Thank you for rescuing me! HalleluYAH, I now experience freedom that I can give pure love and, in return, be loved unconditionally. I will always exalt HIM and praise HIM for the freedom that replaced my prison, and I, now, live with passion.

CHAPTER 6
THE MOVIE THAT LASTS FOR A LIFETIME

The movie starts with a panoramic view of a brownish-red, bricked home, manicured yard with bright, colorful flowers and yellow daisies aligning the driveway. The long driveway ended with a car port that was the main entrance into the home.

Near the right side of the port, there was a blossoming Crape Myrtle Tree filled with bright, pink flowers with the company of two birds on a tree limb, one flying towards the sun. This frame is completely without sound, but with a thick eeriness in the air. An indescribable silence that only a deaf person could understand and feel.

Imagine the camera panning the landscape, slowly, only to lead you inside the house. The first room you enter is a spotless kitchen, glistening appliances. To the left is the living room, carpet undisturbed and all going the same way. It slows down as it crosses the hallway. The camera comes to a closed door and stops!

Through the corridor, to the end of the hallway, it stops at the corner bedroom of the house. From a slightly compromised frame, you see the brightness of the light bursting through the cracks that surrounded the door frame. On the other side of the door, to this day, I find it hard to explain and/or rationalize the events that the world would understand.

I have surrendered my understanding to my purpose and focused my energies to give a sound to my voice that would call out into the deep for others to hear me and find a sense of comfort that they are not alone. There is a search and rescue mission for each and every one of them. For a half of a century, I lived life as the role of the Victim. I would be torn, bruised, battered, and, seemingly, always on the losing side, a day late or a dollar short. Yep, that was me, or should I say, that used to be me.

Well, folks, it is my half time, and I am out of the locker room, geared up, and will be roaring for the next 50 years or so! I am cheering and roaring for you and me! A roar that has been building and stirring for half of a century! Roaring for my mother and father who did not get the chance to roar like the king and queen of jungle that they really were.

I am roaring for my forefathers and foremothers who were deprived of life's civil liberties. I am roaring and taking back all the confidence, along with the rights and privileges, that were stolen from us, a free people, redeemed by YAHUSHA HAMASHIACH, children of the Most High God, YHWH! I am roaring my for Blood-Bought salvation, for my God-given purpose! I am roaring, demonstrating so that all others could glean and gather some form of semblance that they, like me, can and will live a victorious life and not life as a victim. We win in this life and the gates of hell shall not prevail!

Let us take back what was taken from us! Let us take it back by force! Many have pitied us, and some counted us out. Sadly enough, many turned their heads and their hands away from us, because we were victims, but today marks a new day, HALLELUYAH! Join me in saying, "I am no longer victim to my past, hurts, pains, or misunderstandings! I will not be defined or conformed to the darkness and evil this world has to offer. I am transformed by renewing my mind, according to the Love and Truth of YHWH and His Holy Kingdom!"

Join me in living and enjoying what life has to offer through the spectrum of Kingdom living. I encourage and insist you to stop merely existing in a shell of a life that is not truly you and live. I have learned how to live abundantly, and I am more than willing to share with you the knowledge that I have learned. Say it with me, I will live and not die and will declare the works of The Lord. My life is a song, revealing who YHWH IS and WILL ALWAYS BE! Who I am and what I do is to magnify HIS Fullness and HIS Glory. HIS fullness loved me back to life.

I want you to live your life as it was intended, knowing that you are loved and not forgotten, knowing that you have been given assignment on this earth that gives your life meaning, purpose, and fulfillment. Know that joy and happiness are not exclusive to money. Rather, it is inclusive of peace of mind, in a resting place, within your soul, in the abase and the abound.

Let me tell you something, if you are reading this book, you, or someone within your social circle, needs to hear me and join me in everyday living, winning and taking back what was taken from us! Know that the dark forces of this wicked world tried to snuff out our light and annihilate our gifts and talents that were meant for multiplication and spreading through our families and communities, regions, and even the world even.

We have work to do, my sisters and brothers, and we will be the first partakers of the fruit that will be produced! Our Creator has placed principles and laws in the universe that give us all access to define and personify success, wealth, happiness, and wholeness. Come forth with your heart and believe that HE IS YHWH, The Great I Am!

Through confession of the mouth and believing in your heart (read Romans 10:10), accept HIM. We are all connected in this human race and need each other to reach our full potential. I say to you, come out, come out of the darkness that tried its best efforts to silence you, kill you, and destroy you. I know we can live victoriously, and despite your beginning, despite the interruption!

ADREAN MASON

CHAPTER 7
FROM SOMEONE THAT KNOWS

Take it from someone who knows, the worst you can do is to live a lie. Live behind the mask of the great masquerade. I can say this with certainty, because I am telling you my reality that masked itself as my truth. I fooled everyone, I fooled them all with vanity. Meanwhile, the real me, inside, was at constant, cumbersome tug-of-war. A bright smile, body was always a figure 8, no matter what age.

My closest friend of all times would say to me that I could wear a bed sheet and still catch all eyes and be desirable. Money was never a problem for me, and I always had career choices and avenues that afforded me privileges, toys, and trinkets that my heart desired. But, how many of you can relate, that all that glistens and shines is not necessarily gold or good for you?

This world can be quite seductive and misleading when presented in its deceitful luster, designed to keep you entrapped into bondage.

Satan is cunning and always has been, his sole purpose is to present this world laced in power, lust and pride, designed to kill, steal, and destroy the true you. Essentially, living an unrepentant life, you will join the club of the dead, walking about and above ground. You become a junkie, feeding from all that is vanity and empty, void of real happiness and joy. Most of all, it is void of real love and relationship with the Father of Heaven, YHWH!

It's not too late. If you are reading this and want to accept Jesus, YAHUSHUA HAMASHIACH, as your personal Savior, repeat after me: "YAHUSHUA, I know You are real. I believe You are the Son of the Most High GOD; the GOD of Abraham, the GOD of Isaac, and the GOD of Jacob. I believe with all my heart that you sacrificed your life and died for all my past, present and future sin.

It is my belief that GOD Almighty, YHWH, raised You from the dead, and You, now, have all power in your hands. I thank you for saving me, and I know I am now saved, that I may live my eternity with You in Heaven! As I live on this earth, I understand that I am reborn, and my way of thinking, doing, and being will change over time as I learn of You. I, now, open my heart for Your love to flood my soul and give You permission to soothe the pain, hurt, and confusion. I know You have forgiven me for all my sins, and now I will learn how to live healed and free. I know it is a process, and I accept my process because I know that I can get through anything with Your love and guidance. Thank you! I make You LORD of my life. I will hold on to You and learn of You, and become closer to You day by day and, maybe even, hour by hour."

Congratulations!!!! You Did It! You received salvation through your confession and belief in YAHUSHUA HAMASHIACH!

As I look back, chronicling my journey, I can clearly see the trap that was ever so subtle to keep me from doing what you just did, by surrendering to Heavenly Father. I actually thought I was making my life my best life. Every outfit I bought, designer pair of hills I sported, couture blouses, body-con fitted dresses, short and long, natural hair, to the best sew-ins ever, were all part of my wardrobe and makeup to go out everyday and perform.

I put on a good show; I performed what my idea of what I thought happiness and wholeness were to be; a realization that I drew from dramatization, mostly shaped from TV soap operas, nighttime dramas, and childhood fairytales. My my, was I not blinded, because no matter how close I came to look magazine perfect, the moments in between wardrobe changes, I was miserable and did not even want to live.

I knew… if no one else knew, or even cared, for that matter. I was living a lie, and my real life was nothing of what I dressed up and pretended to be. In fact, it was the exact opposite. There is such a blessing in the simplicity of life. (PRAISE BREAK)! I have a joy that is indescribable and peace that goes beyond my understanding!

CHAPTER 8
IT HAPPENS OVER TIME

It did not happen overnight; it happens over time. It was a process, including stages and levels of healing and growth. I assure you, you will be pleased, just as I am, with who you have become and continue to grow into today. Guess what…it ain't over. Life keeps getting better and better. I survived and now I thrive!

Once upon a time, my life was the personification of sad, depressed, and suicidal, but never would have termed myself as a victim because of the stigma associated with it. I stayed away from the victim terminology because of the weight of what this word entailed. To me, being a victim meant the end of living a normal life, and I did not want to be abnormal. It was important for me to be like everyone else.

I was mistaken and, now, I gladly accept that I am peculiar and that I live a life of freedom and reassurance. Before accepting who, GOD made me to be, I struggled with the daunting memories that constantly played on a loop reel, awake or sleep. It was my lifeline to be normal and pretend that those things did not impact me.

Lord knows, being normal was especially important to me, and I was willing to live a life that portrayed me as normal rather pronounced as abnormal, aka, a "victim". Now, in this moment in time, moving forward, I can honestly say that being a victim does not mean you die in the attack.

To me, being the victim of heinous acts meant that the devil tried his best shot and lost the bet. I did not die. He could not kill me. He could not destroy what did not belong to him. HalleluYAH, I survived the attack(s), and now I thrive!

For all victims that can read or hear this message, if you have endured an attack in your life, whether from childhood or just a short while ago, let's not hang our heads in defeat as poor victims. I stand with you. Let's raise our heads and lift our voices, send notice to the world that we are the kind of victims that are fighting back and, not only fighting back, we are taking back everything that was stolen, broken, or covered up!

World, hear us roar, feel our force, and get ready for our passion to thrive. We do and will continue to make impact everywhere our feet tread. Watch the transformation from Victim to Victor!

You are probably asking the question, *how do we begin this transformation*? I am glad you asked that question. It was not easy for me, but as a living witness, I know it is doable. I had to start with these: commitment discipline, and the vow to complete this book even in its toughest and darkest hour. Warning: know, from the beginning that you will have to revisit places and dig up bones that you would rather them stay covered up. It is a must, however, to reach your place of healthy living, that you must have, to reach your abundant living. Know that it will make others uncomfortable that would prefer you just "leave it in the past," but every person that says that does not know your restless nights and wrestle with death. Ignore their words, follow the voice that abides within, and keep moving towards your healthy, wealthy place.

Be committed and vow that you will keep going when it seems like you have reached the toughest and darkest hour. Keep going! There is victory on the other side of this fight. Everything that was stolen, lost, and traded in is on the other side of this.

Walk with me as I escort you through my journey of finally coming to terms that I was a victim. That realization was critical in my transformational process, becoming and walking into my freedom and abundance. I am no longer existing, but living my life and not some fabricated, Hollywood story. In the chronicle order of events and seasons in my life, it spelled out the acronym V-I-C-T-I-M. I opened this book to where all of it began for me, the interruption of the master's grand plan for my life. It was the invasion, the hostile takeover, or simply said, the Violation that tried its best to claim my best life.

CHAPTER 9
V: VIOLATION

    I can still see the little girl. She is four years old, sitting flat on the floor with her knees close to her little chest. Her arms are wrapped as tight as she can hold her little body. Her dolls are scattered on the floor, now far from her reach. Hair shuffled, clothes unsecured on her little body, and her front hair bow missing. Dried up tear tracks on her face.

    There is no sound coming from her mouth. She is staring out into the deep of her room, remaining unresponsive. Rocking back and forth, back and forth. Baby Girl, Baby Girl, can you hear me? Hold on, I am sorry, I'm so sorry no one came to your rescue. Hold on, please, this is not your fault. Hold on Baby Girl, fight, fight to come back to me, you can do it, come back to me!

I see her. It hurts so badly to see her and cannot defend her. She is just a little girl. Lord, it hurts to see the little girl left in this state. She is not even mentally developed at age four to conceive what just happened to her. She has been violated. Oh GOD, where are You, where were You, and why did you let this happen to me?

These are very real questions that I am sure I am not the only one that has ever posed to YHWH ALMIGHTY. This does not make any sense to me or that little girl. And the woman I am today, admittedly, has struggled most of my life with the tell of this story.

Violated by the one that was supposed to protect her, provide for her, teach her right from wrong, walk her down the aisle, give her away at her wedding, play with his grandchildren, and give them ice cream and cookies. And not be the one that served up a dish of torment for her to feed on for the next four decades to follow.

From that moment following the violation, I was flooded by an invasion that I describe as a hostile takeover. The villain forced his way into my life, robbing me of a normal childhood, darkening my teenage years and frazzling my adult life as a mother and as a wife. His intention was to thrust me into an existence that was not mine. A life that would never agree and align with the original blueprint of greatness and effectiveness. A life that would toil because of the misalignment, to the point of suicide.

It was as though my little body was rolled tightly to be shot from a cannon, to be catapulted into a waste field, a land filled with the most unwanted, undesirable, and uninhabitable junk.

Picture this, I was shot from a cannon as part of some sick circus act, shot into a foreign land with all the same people, only now, they all speak a different language than I do. How am I supposed to navigate through this land filled with sharp edged objects at every turn?

It was too much for me, I was only four years old. Even my adult self struggles with this as my reality. I did not know what to do. I did not know how to feel. I did not know what to say.

A four-year-old would not have the mental maturity, in development, to understand, much less, process what had happened. In all its horror, perhaps, an adult could grasp at the weight of such horror, but I was not an adult, I was a child. A child that understands clean up time, mealtime, bath time, happy and sad, but not capable of understanding how to process the shattering from the evil vibrations of sick molestation. That four-year-old did what she could: pulled her knees to her chest, wrap her arms around her little legs, and just hold on, rocking back and forth.

Hold on, Baby Girl! One great day, this will pass and make sense. This violation was sent on a mission to destroy me, and is being used as the vehicle in my life's work that will glorify the relationship that matters, trusting and believing in YHWH's overall plan to heal mankind.

I am determined that this violation will not define who I AM or who I am to become: it was, however, an impacting fact that appeared in my timeline here on earth, but it will not be my truth! The force behind the villain's tactics thought he had me. I am certain, in the stretch of my imagination it reported back to its evil general, *we got us another one that will not live out her potential.*

He probably laughed, and jokingly reported, *I left her barely alive, her body will heal but I damaged her mind, heart and soul. That will never heal.* HAHA! But, it just did not know, I had been given a Helper, authority, and power on the final laugh and say so in my life. HALLELUYAH, it's been a long time coming, but I AM Back, and back with the greatest Force of all forces, the Force beyond anything natural. Watch the transformation!

ADREAN MASON

CHAPTER 10
I: ISOLATION

You are not alone. I need you to, truly, know that you are not in this by yourself. I know it very much feels like you are alone and have been abandoned by those closest to you. Unable to process and unable to speak about it, it becomes overwhelming, choking even to the point of anxiety. The fear becomes crippling.

Who can you trust? Who can you confide in? Weighed down by burdens that cannot be articulated. Shame becomes your second skin and affects every area of your life; your health, physical appearance, speech, and mental capacity, It also affects you academically, socially, and interpersonally. It begins a deterioration that can only be stopped by confronting it head on.

How can I confront this head on by myself? This was the plot of the villain to leave me feeling like

I was all on my own and have no one to turn to. The enemy does its job effectively, it is committed and disciplined in using his devices, speaking lies into your hearing. Here are some things that I heard repeatedly, over and over and over, to the point of frustration and desperation.

I would grow up listening to these and eventually believing it in my subconscious. These thoughts filled my mental space and left little room for positive and pure thoughts. It painted a poor picture of the real me that I, eventually, adopted as my reality. Thoughts such as, "Are you sure that happened?" "No one will believe you", "You asked for it", "You are fast and brought this on yourself". These phrases built a wall around me, a wall built of isolation.

Isolation is prime real estate for the enemy forces. You get tired of fighting. You get tired of the voices surrounding your head. They wait for you in your dreams, they are there when you wake up.

There is no rest for you. I was unable to speak, left in a complete speechless fog. No words can be formed to describe a child being sexually abused and violated, persuaded that it was okay to let it happen. It disagreed with every fiber inside of me, left me powerless, conflicted and confused. My foundation of trust and love would be shattered to unrecognizable pieces. It destroys and rewrites what you have learned as right versus wrong, light versus dark, good vs evil. There is no longer a sense of balance in the universe, and it changes how you view and hear anyone or anything ever again.

It was forbidden to kill me, so it settled for second best, to try to kill the me that I was to become. It was strategic in efforts to slightly crack my cup, causing a steady leak that would never allow the cup to fill and reach full capacity. Its plan was to make me a half-empty-cup kind of person that would never see the cup/glass half full. I could only see the glass half full for others, never for myself. I was shaped to believe that I was unworthy of real love, joy, and happiness.

The years to come, are scattered, blanks for me that I uncovered across psychotherapy sessions. For the most part, I was left with unsettling events that occurred to me. One scattered memory, I was in the bedroom closet silently crying, hiding under his work clothes that reeked of his body odor, sweat, salt, cheap deodorant, and motor oil. I can smell it even now.

Another detached memory is when I was summoned to sit on the side of his bed after getting in trouble for stealing my older sister's red fingernail polish. Mom worked in the afternoons, 3pm-11pm. I sat on the side of the bed, and I can see him looking at me, in my eyes, as though he was hypnotizing me as he slid his finger down the back of my pants. NOOOOOOO, please stop, the bombshell of the memories will never go away. You just learn to manage it.

Before I learned how to manage my pain and emotions, the recall of any direct or indirect events triggered a reliving of the actual pain, the mental thwart, and the physical pain of the intrusion. It was as if it placed me back in time to relive it, both as the child and now as an adult. I remember the pain in my vaginal cavity. I can remember blacking out, awakening to a state of suffocation and panic you can only imagine. How do you cry out… and to whom?

I bottled my fear, and the bottle filled up. I used a bigger container as I grew older, through adolescence, the teenage years, young adult years, as well as through motherhood. These containers became my urns that followed me everywhere I went; into every job, every relationship, every church, every business idea, and every project. I was surrounded by so many that depended upon me as a teacher, supervisor, parent, and spouse.

It does not make sense. On the outside, my life was fulfilled and sparkling, with cosmopolitan success. I knew I lived a life in isolation that was the furthest from fulfillment and joy. I performed quite well, had them all fooled. Everyone I served got what they needed and wanted. I was the one left barren and empty, without connection. There was no connection strong enough that could reach deep within my soul to quench my thirst and satisfy my hunger.

When is my turn, Oh LORD, I would ask? My cry was, *I'm so tired LORD YAHUSHUA. It is time to scatter these ashes and leave them at sea for good. I am tired of crying; there are no more tears. Now what?*

ADREAN MASON

CHAPTER 11
C: CONFLICTED

Sexually abused, emotionally stripped, and spiritually dehydrated, I was left numb and void of trust and love. At such a young age, I had no cognitive relationship with GOD, The Father, Jesus, The Son, or the Holy Spirit. My most loved, bigger-than-life, personality was, probably, Captain Kangaroo. My biggest challenge, probably, was putting the clothes on my dolls correctly. So, when the invasion and devastation came in like a tidal wave and overshadowed my four-year-old self, it was targeting the me I Am to become. This devastation left me comfortless and conflicted.

It saw an advantage to attack me at the stage of pre-k development, while I knew extraordinarily little of anything. Basically, you are a clean slate available for the impressions of life to make its imprint, and anxious to shape your mind and heart. During these formative years, it is a race and fight between good versus evil, darkness versus light, depression versus freedom, live versus die, and victim versus victor!

Strategically, it presented itself as the mastery interruption in my developmental growth, to cause infractions in my ability to relate, trust, and connect with people. At four years old, I could not scientifically absorb or handle what happened to me. Literally, my frontal lobe was not developed. It is the area of the brain that controls the important, cognitive skills in humans, such as emotional expression, problem solving, memory, language, judgment, and sexual behaviors. It is the "control panel" of our personality and our ability to communicate.

The frontal lobe reaches it maturity at the approximate age of 25. The ruler of darkness sends out his imps with vices of destruction at a young age in order to warp and crack your foundation, contaminating your root system. His wicked hope is that everything that will grow and pass through your contaminated root system will be twisted and produce corrupt fruit that would repeatedly produce its own kind, corrupt fruit.

Remember in an earlier chapter, I mentioned that the universe has been given irrevocable orders? These orders are equipped with principles and laws that are to produce plentifully, for all that would make them applicable and practical in their lives. Mankind has been given a gift, a command to be fruitful and multiply, replenish the earth, subdue it, and have dominion over every living thing that move upon the earth. You were designed to conquer, dominate, rule, and reign. Satan's plan was to render me comfortless and hopeless. Glory to GOD for being sovereign. His Love drew me back. His Patience provided a comfort I cannot explain. His Revealed Plan gave me strength to fight and the fight to win!

ADREAN MASON

CHAPTER 12
T: TOILING

From my first memory to now, I have had to fight and toil to keep myself afloat. Truth be told, by the time I reached my twenties, I was torn ragged and worn down so low that I had to look up to see an ant pass by. From ages four to twenty-one, my memories are few and far between battles that I lost. In adolescence, I was a mute for 5 years. Staring and crying were my primary language, eventually opening with a severe, stuttered speech.

I was known to start small fires, named "pyromaniac" by my siblings, and excluded from the neighborhood parties and sleepovers. In my teenage years, I had run away from home in the eighth grade, tried to seduce one of my middle school teachers (it failed), and as I was introduced to my high school teen years, I was secretly promiscuous.

ADREAN MASON

By the time I was sent away to college, I was attracted to the risky crowd, bad boys, those that dabbled in drugs, drinking, and sex. Although I was sure to stay close to such a crowd, there was something that kept me from the drugs and the drinking. That something would be the plan that GOD had for me.

I led two different lives, I was a Dean's list student in the day, only by night to be controlled by a hunger to be loved that would allow men, married or single, my age or near senior citizen, black or white, to deposit their trash and keep going. All undercover. I pretended not to care, but then I cried when no one was around. Longing to be loved, I compromised my values and ignored boundaries, trying to convince everyone to love me.

I can remember being so tired and exhausted of living two lives. The opinion of myself was not healthy at all. I believed I was meant to be someone's doormat, left outside to catch dirt, dog poop, leaves, and trash, a buffer between the outside grime and rodents that tried to make their way in to enter the owner's home. Torn apart by the emptiness that invaded my existence, my constant cry was, "Will anyone ever notice me? Will anyone want to be in a relationship with me, love me, cherish me, marry me…anyone?" "Why am I not lovable GOD?" "What am I doing wrong?"

I was not getting any answers to my questions, which made me angry and more reckless in my actions. No answers to me, at that time, meant to intensify what I was doing and maybe situations will change in my favor. How twisted is that frame of thinking? Not a response from GOD, especially when you are doing all the wrong things that are out of the Will of GOD.

My kindled anger would begin to shatter the already thin connection of trust and love with The One who created me. I did not learn until much later in life that I had lost trust in YHWH. I was angry with the world, and my toiling turned into a cyclone that was destroying everything in sight.

ADREAN MASON

CHAPTER 13
I: INSANITY

I am so tired, Oh LORD, would be my words, crying deep into the night, as I prayed to just be able to fall asleep and rest without the nightmare of my life's mistakes playing on a replay loop. An all too familiar cry, even into my late-thirties and early forties.

I was frustrated beyond words could express. I am responsible for a whole other human being that is defenseless in this world at such a young age. It was my duty to keep her safe and protected from the evil of this world. I am somebody's mother and struggled with my own self-worth. How could I teach her? Would I be convincing enough to her, even though I did not believe the very words I was saying?

I remember going to church one Sunday, with the intentions of going to the altar, because someone, probably a mother of the old-time church and/or the new age church, told me to lay my problems at the altar and give them to GOD. Well, I went to the altar and started to pour out my heart. The tears began to stream into a steady flow. Ushers pushed tissue into my hands, it did not help the flood. The carpeted altar step beneath me would capture most of this mucous-filled water flow, streaming from my face and nose. I could not stop crying. My hairpiece fell from my head, I did not care, I continued to cry and cry aloud.

I cried out to GOD through devotion, I cried through praise and worship, I cried through announcements, right there on the floor, left of the pulpit. Ushers came to move me, for it was time for the Pastor to preach. My crying intensified. A gate had been let open, and I could not close it.

You see, by this time, I had been married a few years and miserable! I was married to a man that was just as broken as I was, and he knew less of what to do with me than I did. I do not fault him, in fact, I apologized to him. I married him thinking he was the answer to all my problems and the glue to my every broken place in my life, from four years to that point in time. That was unreasonable thinking, but at the time that I said I do, I was thinking this is it! As far back as I could remember, my behavior pattern was very predictable. I would repeat the same behaviors and actions, but expecting different results. That is the classic definition of insanity.

I had given my body to the point in which it held no thrills for me. I had offered up my heart in every encounter, to the point of hopelessness, and the only thing I had left was my mind, until that one day, it snapped. What would bring me back? Could something or someone bring me back?

My life was becoming a picture of insanity without the certification from a physician. Until, one day would come that I would be contained in a hospital room, monitored by a camera and armed-police guards, later to be Sheriff-escorted to a mental facility for a three-day suicide watch. There would be 3 more documented nervous break downs. *I am tired, Oh Lord, help me. I do not know what to do!* I had nothing else to offer the world. Now, a mother, I wanted to live for my child, I just did not know how to live in the liberty of YAHUSHUA HAMASHIACH. I had to learn how to walk in my authority and dominion.

ADREAN MASON

CHAPTER 14
M: MOUNTAINS DO MOVE

I, now, know that mountains are moved, but, until one year ago, my belief was supported by the limitations of the world's explanation. The world told me only the skilled and trained can conquer a mountain, so the rest of us are to just take it as a defeat and settle to live at the bottom of the mountain. There is a song I remember from my childhood with the following lyrics, "I'm coming up on the rough side of the mountain." That sounds overwhelming and exhausting to me.

I imagine that the fact of having a mountain before me is intimidating, and to have no other route, other than the rough side of the mountain, is too much for me to bear. Metaphorically speaking, I understand exactly what the songwriter was saying. As I look back, I have found myself left without options in the moment. What I understand now, I was not supposed to crumble in the fear, rather, I was to swell with belief in the truth and keep stepping forward, trusting that YHWH will be YWHW as I trust in HIM to do so.

I have proven that, when you rely on GOD to be GOD, you encounter HIS miracles, provision, and peace. Lean not on your own understanding, trade in your anxiety and nervous break downs for peace and strength to endure and overcome. Stop limiting GOD and reducing HIM to human efforts. I tell you, there are mountains marked fear, anxiety, anger, rejection, abandonment, loneliness, lack, poverty, and debt, forming a line of defense to keep you from your destiny and wealthy place.

In most cases, they are unavoidable. Run to them with your confession of faith, that YHWH is a mountain mover. HE shall escort you through your journey. In the moment you feel like throwing in the towel, hang on to it a little while longer and begin to wave it to the LORD, GOD ALMIGHTY. Tell HIM thank you for leveling the mountain for you. Begin to tell your obstacle how big your GOD is! Plead your case, make your petition known, cry unto Him to show up on your behalf and be that very present help proclaimed in His Word.

Faith is a force that will prove that mountains do move! Faith without movement towards the expectation is reducing faith to rubbing a genie bottle at a carnival. Where is the work, your work toward your desired result of what you are believing for? Faith is asking for clients, while building the business. Build it, and they will come.

Faith is pushing forward through a nervous breakdown and being rejected by the bank over 300 times before one finally says, *yes*. We know his works as Walt Disney.

Faith is pushing forward after being turned down by MGM Studios. Fred Astaire's audition report card had comments that he was bald, looked funny and could dance only a little.

Faith is continuing to apply for the nursing program after several denials, through a journey of, 8 years later, now serving in the healthcare industry with a PHD.

Faith is pushing through academic probation to become a current day graduate, certified and licensed as a Registered Nurse, passing the state exam, NCLEX, in the 1st attempt.

Faith is continuing to push forward, believing in your dream, performing in your own written and self-produced play of six failed attempts and believing it will be successful, and becoming the highest paid man in entertainment in 2011. He earned over $130 million from 2010-2011. Today, Tyler Perry owns over 300 acres of, once former confederate land, and built a state-of-the-art studio, larger than Hollywood's.

Faith is pushing beyond sleeping in your car, homeless for three years, earning $50 a week in 1993 to journey to 2019 with a net worth of $160 million. He hosts his own TV show, is a popular radio host, and is a best-selling author. We know him as Steve Harvey.

It is time for our bio to become newsworthy. It is time to start the project, write the vision, and make it plain, with monthly objectives and weekly goals. Finish the book, one chapter at a time. I encourage you to move forward, despite the height or width of the mountains before you. Its size is insignificant, because the power to move it is activated by your force of faith not your physical strength.

CHAPTER 15
FORCE IN ACTION

Believe me when I say, this year, I was ready for them. I expected the mountains to present themselves. I anticipated a few land mines along the way and was careful to take steps, that were ordered by GOD, to avoid the explosions. Coming to terms that being a victim was not the end of me but was my process toward the intentional me. Do not fight the process, embrace it and learn of YHWH, The Father, The Son and The Holy Spirit.

Seek the Holy Word for your answers. To learn scripture is to learn of Him, and He will reveal His plan for your life. All the pieces of your puzzled life will begin to come together, and it will be for the good. His plan is to truly prosper you and bring you to an expected end. He has called you blessed, highly favored, the head and not the tail, above always, and not beneath. Do not go by what you see in your sight, you must know and hang onto what He has said.

Your circumstances are merely facts that have occurred on your timeline here on earth, but I encourage you to learn of your truth. Truth is established in The Holy Word. He has provided you with The Way to spend eternity with Him. He has declared to make your name great among the nations. He has given you an inheritance. He has given you a purpose. He has made provision for your health and wealth. Fear not, He has not given you the spirit of fear, but has given you power, love, and a sound mind! Now, grow in your faith! Use your faith with the force of the Holy Ghost Power!

Speak the Holy Word, as recorded by Matthew 17:20. YAHUSHUA, Himself, instructs us to speak directly to the mountain, using our faith, commanding it to move, and telling it where to go. I moved mine from my land and my family's land, and I moved them into the deepest sea, never to return. I declare war, with the blessed reassurance that ABBA FATHER, GOD ALMIGHTY, fights my battles and upholds me with His right arm. He is the LORD of Hosts; He dispatches His angelic army on my behalf.

I proclaim victory against these mountains formed as weapons against me, they have been removed, and the land has been leveled for me to run through with all momentum. My faith is set on the reaching of the other side. My promise land is on the other side. HALLELUYAH!

Stay the course! Remember, your momentum is fueled from the stint of being a victim. In fact, being a victim has qualified you to win. Win to help others out of the pit that could easily swallow them whole. Repeat after me, there will not be a repeat defeat for me. I have the victory!

ABOUT THE AUTHOR

Adrean Mason offers readers a collected view that provides a bridge to YHWH that engages and activates practical application of the Holy principles to one of life's "lump in your throat" moments. It turns into a message of deliverance and freedom. This book offers the spiritual underpinnings of applying Kingdom principles of Christianity as a tool and guide to set those captives free from the depths and darkness of depression. It illuminates a personal path to The Way, The Truth, and The Life!

As a voice to all those stranded in the deep and darkness of molestation, Adrean shares a true story that will help readers make sense of the ruins of the past, manage the rubble of the present, and begin to take control and navigate to the promise of a future they can look forward to. Using wisdom, collected from more than 30 years of serving others as an educator and marketplace leader and entrepreneur, Adrean shows how life's spiritual awareness and transformation enriches and illuminates life's path that guides one to a fulfilling purpose; freedom and joy. This is a must read for those that want to break free of life's cyclic battle of low self-esteem and depression.

An inspirational S.O.S. lifeboat, *No Longer Bound*, knows from experience how to dive into the deep reaches, take hold of you, and bring you to the surface so that you can begin to breathe again and make it in to shore. Unafraid of your kicking and screaming, you can count on Adrean Mason to provide realistic support, free of the empty clichés, that will lead to an inner peace, confidence, and trust. You have a lot to live for! Live your life! Live no longer bound!

Made in the USA
Columbia, SC
02 September 2020